Contents

Keanu playing with his band Dog Star.

1 Why is Keanu Reeves a star?

He turns down big films
to be in a play on the stage,
or play with his band Dog Star.

Some of the films he does make
are not smash hits.

He doesn't act like a Hollywood star.
He doesn't go to Hollywood parties.
Most of all,
he doesn't even want to be a star.

He has even said,
'I don't want to be super famous.
That would be awful.'

Keanu doesn't want to be a star.
He doesn't have a big flashy house
or a big flashy car.
He lives in hotels
and rides a 1974 Norton motorbike.

Maybe his fans love him
because of this.
They love him because he is ordinary
and different at the same time.
It is not easy
to say what kind of person he is.
He is not easy to pin down.

Keanu rides a 1974 Norton motorbike.

2 Early years

Even his childhood years
were a mixture
of ordinary and different.

His mother is English.
His father is half Hawaiian and half Chinese.

Keanu was born in Lebanon in 1964.
He was given a Hawaiian name.
It means 'the coolness'.
It's a name for a man or a woman.
Just right
for the actor you can't pin down.

His parents split up
when Keanu and his sister Kim were little.

His mother, Patric,
took her children to New York.
She married Paul, a film director.
They went to live in Canada.
Keanu Charles Reeves
took up Canadian citizenship.
He is still a Canadian citizen today.

Patric and Paul split up a year later.
But Keanu always stayed
in touch with his step-father Paul.

Patric went on to marry again
and have another baby called Karina.

Each time a different man
came into his mum Patric's life,
the family moved.
Keanu changed school almost every year.

He was dyslexic
and left-handed,
so school was even harder for him.

His mother made expensive clothes
for rich and famous stars.
So Keanu was used to seeing famous people,
like David Bowie and Alice Cooper,
in his house.

Keanu's childhood was very different
to other children's lives,
but he also did ordinary things.

Keanu loved playing ice hockey.
He was so good at school
that he could have been professional.

3 First films

Keanu had another interest
and that was acting.

He acted at the schools he went to,
and in the holidays he flew to LA
to stay with his step-father Paul.
He hung around on the film sets
as his step-father worked.

Back in Canada
Keanu changed school again.
This time he went to an acting school.
He went straight into the top class.

The school did a show in 1983.
An agent saw the 18-year-old Keanu
and signed him up.
She got him a lot of work
doing TV adverts.

Keanu liked to be scruffy.
But it was not trendy to be scruffy
at that time in Canada.
His agent tried to make him a bit smarter.
It didn't work.

But it didn't matter.
He still got the parts.

In 1984,
he got his first small film part.
He played an ice hockey player
in a comedy called *Young Blood*.

It was an awful film
but at least it was a start.

In the spring of the next year,
Keanu was chosen
to be in a Disney film.
He went to LA
for the film *Young Again*.

It was one of the first films
to get him noticed.

In Canada at that time
the film industry was small.
So there weren't many parts.
Keanu solved this problem
by driving to LA in 1986
in his 20-year-old Volvo car.

This time he stayed.

At first he lived with his step-father Paul.
Then he got himself a new agent
and rented a flat.

Keanu was given parts
in four films for TV.
But he wanted to do more
than just TV work.

He got a part in the film *River's Edge*.
It's the film of a real event:
the murder of a young girl.
The film showed
the dark side of America.

It was a surprise hit
and the critics liked Keanu.

In 1987 in Hollywood
there was a big talent search.
A film company was making a film
called *Bill and Ted's Excellent Adventure*,
and they were looking for actors.

Many actors wanted to be in this film.
In the end Keanu and Alex Winter
were chosen.

The film was a comedy
about two school kids, Bill and Ted.
Keanu played Ted.
The kids are no good at history lessons.
But then they are given
a time-travel machine.

Bill and Ted go back in time
in the machine.
They bring back famous people
to help them
with their history home work.

The film was not seen for two years.
The critics said it was bad.
But it was a success
at the box office
and went on to make a lot of money.

Some of Bill and Ted's words from the film
were used by young people
all over the world.
Words like 'Bogus', 'Dude',
and 'Most Excellent!'

Keanu and Alex Winter in *Bill and Ted's Excellent Adventure*.

4 Choosing films

After making eight films,
among them *River's Edge* and *Bill and Ted*,
Keanu could choose the films he made.
He turned down *The Fly II*,
and chose a part in a costume drama.

Keanu was in hospital
when he found out that he had a small part
in *Dangerous Liaisons*.
He had crashed his motorbike.
(He still has a long scar down his body
from that crash.)

Dangerous Liaisons
is a film about sex, power and money.
Keanu plays a young man
who is used by others
as part of their cruel games.

Keanu was unhappy
with his acting on *Dangerous Liaisons*
Critics said he looked out of place.

It was proving hard for Keanu
to get away from playing
young American dudes.

He was worried
that Ted would be the only part
people would remember him for.

By the late 1980s,
Keanu was finally moving away
from playing parts like Ted.

He played a hit man
in *I Love You To Death*.

On this film
he met River Phoenix.
River wasn't in the film
but his girlfriend was.
River and Keanu were to be good friends
for the next six years.

Keanu's career took off slowly
because he chose to be
in films that were different.

5 Taking off

In 1990,
his career began to take off.
In seven months
he starred in three films.

The first was a thriller
called *Point Break*.
He played an FBI agent,
the same age as himself, 25.
This agent joined a gang of surfers
who were robbing banks.

Keanu went to Hawaii
to learn surfing.
He didn't have time to become an expert.
But that didn't matter
because in the film
he spends a lot of time falling off!

Point Break
was one of the more successful films
of 1991.

They finished filming after 77 days.
Keanu flew at once to Oregon,
to start filming
My Own Private Idaho.

In this film
Keanu played a rich boy,
who becomes a rent boy,
to spite his father.
River Phoenix played his friend,
another rent boy.

Keanu and River had been friends
for over six years.
They were happy working together.

They were both
'flower children' of the 60s.
River's family
had put him in films when he was nine
because they were short of money.
Keanu's family had let him do
what he wanted to do.

Keanu worked on his part
in *My Own Private Idaho*
by reading books.
River was a method actor.
He worked on his part
by living the part.
He may have gone too far with drugs.

It was a difficult film
for both actors.
The critics gave most praise to River.

6 A flop and three hits

A very tired Keanu
went on to make
Bill and Ted's Bogus Journey.
He kept his hair long,
so that it hid his tired eyes.

In this film
Bill and Ted travel to Heaven and Hell.
They make friends with Death
and they all play Twister together.

Bill and Ted's Bogus Journey
was supposed to be a blockbuster.
It wasn't.
In fact, it was a bit of a flop.

But *Point Break* was a big hit with the fans.
And *My Own Private Idaho*
became a classic.

After three films Keanu needed a rest.
He said 'I'm a basket case.'

Keanu didn't get a rest.
He rushed into making
Bram Stoker's *Dracula*.
But he was lifeless in the film.

Keanu in *Point Break*.

The critics said
he looked like he'd lost all his blood
before the film started.
He said 'I didn't act well.'

So he took a rest
and didn't act
until the next year, 1992.

Keanu had been in Shakespeare's plays
on the stage.
A part in *Much Ado About Nothing*
gave him his chance
to be in a Shakespeare play on film.

It was made in Italy
and Keanu played the part of Don John.

Don John is the strong silent type.
In the story he makes problems
for everyone.

The film was a hit
at the box office.
It made $48 million world-wide.

That same year
Keanu also made *The Little Buddha*.
He plays Prince Siddharta
a young man
who has never left home.
He doesn't know the meaning
of old age or sickness.

One day, aged 29,
the same age as Keanu,
he leaves home to travel and learn.
Prince Siddharta
becomes the Buddha.

The film was made
in America, Bhutan and Nepal.
Keanu loved being in Bhutan.
He felt free,
no-one knew him.

In the film
Keanu changed his looks many times.
To film the part where the Buddha fasted
he ate nothing but oranges
and became very thin.

The Little Buddha
could have been a mistake for Keanu.

He wasn't Asian.

Did he have any right
to play a holy man?
But he carried it off with grace.

7 Success and sadness

1993 was a big year for Keanu.
He had great success
and suffered great sadness.

In the film *Speed*
Keanu plays a SWAT agent.
(SWAT is short for
Special Weapons and Technical Unit.)
The story takes place on a speeding bus.

If the speed of the bus
drops below 50 mph
then it would blow up.
The SWAT agent has to save the day.

Eight weeks into filming
Keanu heard that River Phoenix had died
from a drugs overdose.
He was 23.

Keanu said later,
'I think of it as an accident.
I can't make sense of it.'

Speed was the big success
of that summer.
It made $330 million world-wide.
Keanu had finally got rid of Ted.

Just as the film came out
Keanu's real father
was sent to prison for ten years
for possession of drugs.

For years,
Keanu had been angry with his father.
Now he was even more angry.

Keanu in *Johnny Mnemonic*. He played a man who could remember electronic data because he had a micro-chip in his head!

8 A flop and a romance

His next film was a big flop.
It was called
Johnny Mnemonic.

A mnemonic
is a special way
of remembering information.
Keanu played a man
who could remember electronic data
because he had a micro-chip
in his head!

The critics said
the film was flatter than a floppy disc.

Keanu went on to his next film
A Walk in the Clouds.
It was to be
his first great romantic lead.

Keanu played a GI
coming home from World War II.
The GI agrees to pose as the husband
of a pregnant woman
whom he meets on a bus.

Keanu and Aitana Sanchez-Gijon in *A Walk in the Clouds*.

In the film they go back
to her family's vineyard in California
and he really falls in love with her.

When it came out in 1995
the critics said
it was sweet and old fashioned.
It made money
but it was not a blockbuster.

It seemed as if Keanu's career
was going down hill.

He didn't have an Oscar.
He wasn't a method actor,
like the others of his age group.

In fact he wasn't like them at all.
Different might not mean better.

Keanu took off with his band, Dog Star.
In the summer of 1995
they did a tour of America and Japan.

This was a rest from films
for Keanu.

His next film,
as usual, was an odd choice.
He could have made *Speed II*
but he turned down the $11 million.
The film he chose instead was
Feeling Minnesota.

In this film
Keanu plays a small time crook.
The crook falls in love
with his brother's wife
on their wedding day.

The film allowed Keanu
to be more natural
than he was in his last two films.

9 Ordinary or different?

On tour with Dog Star
Keanu had put on kilos in weight
He had to lose them
for his part in *Chain Reaction*.

Keanu got $7 million
plus a share of the profit for this film.
He plays one of two scientists.

Chain Reaction
is a big action film.
The story starts with a bang
as the scientists' lab blows up.
The scientist Keanu plays
gets away on a motorbike.

Keanu made another film in 1996.
It was called
The Last Time I Committed Suicide.
It's a dramatic film
based on a story told in a letter
written from one friend to another.

Also in 1996
he had another motorbike crash.
This time he broke his ankle.

Keanu in *Chain Reaction*.

In his latest film
Keanu co-stars with Al Pacino.
It's called *Devil's Advocate*.
Al Pacino plays the devil
in human form.
He hires Keanu as his lawyer
to do his dirty work.

As well as writing
new songs for Dog Star
Keanu is thinking about a new film.
He has been offered a part
in *Object of my Affection*.
The part is that of a gay man
who has an affair with a woman.

In 1994
gossips said that Keanu
got married to another man.
In 1997 they said
he was engaged
to an English woman
who is already married.

Keanu keeps everyone guessing.

He is not easy to pin down.
His friend Alex Winter says
'He has yet to show people
what he can do.'